Joe Junior

and the Wheels of Steel

written by Carol Day
illustrated by Braden Hallett

First published in paperback by
Michael Terence Publishing in 2023
www.mtp.agency

ISBN 9781800946859

Illustrations and book design by
Braden Hallett

DEDICATION

For Stuart, for always believing in me.

A big thank you to Adam McEvoy and the Wheelchair FA for their help and advice. To all those amazing footballers who play Wheelchair / Powerchair football at all levels, this is for you. To everyone who continues to support Joe Junior and his adventures...thank you !!

ACKNOWLEDGMENTS

With thanks to Braden Hallett for bringing Joe Junior to life for his latest adventure.

"Joe loves football as much as I do. His enthusiasm is infectious, and this book is a joy to read for both children and parents. Joe Junior is perfect for young football fans"

Stuart Pearce MBE

It's Friday afternoon and Joe Junior is sat in the café on the High Street with his mum, Lilly. Max the dog is lying sound asleep under the table by their feet.

Joe has a big mug of hot chocolate on the table in front of him. He has worked really hard at school this week so he is allowed a special treat... a delicious slice of cake.

Joe is sat waiting for his steaming mug of chocolate to cool down and is just about to bite into his cake when the café door bursts open.

The bell above the café door jingles. A young boy, not much older than Joe Junior, wheels himself into the café with a whoop and a spin... nearly knocking Joe's drink off the table and waking up Max the dog.

"I am so sorry," the young boy says apologetically, stopping to check if Joe is ok.

He starts to laugh when he sees the look of surprise on Joe's face. "I don't usually make such a big entrance," he explains still giggling. "It's just that I am super excited."

Max the dog jumps up, his tail wagging, eager to meet their new friend. "I'm Eddie," he says introducing himself.

"What are you so excited about?" Joe asks, smiling at Eddie's enthusiasm. "I made the Football Team!!" he explains, clearly delighted with his news.

Joe couldn't hide his surprise.

Eddie grins. "I can tell by the look on your face that you are not sure how I can play football when I am in a wheelchair?"

"I was wondering," admits Joe.

"It's simple really. I play Wheelchair Football, or you might have heard it called Powerchair Football," explains Eddie proudly.

Joe Junior is really impressed. "I have never heard of Wheelchair or Powerchair Football before," he admits. "It sounds really cool." Max the dog is excited too. Footballs are one of his favourite things.

"Where is your pitch?" questions Joe, "don't your wheels get muddy on the grass?"

Eddie doubles over in his chair laughing.

"Muddy wheels are not a problem," he answers. "We don't play on grass, we use the sports hall at the leisure centre."

Joe's cheeks turn red, feeling silly having asked the question. "Don't worry," says Eddie kindly, "not everyone knows about Wheelchair Football."

"It's not the first time I have been asked about muddy wheels," he says smiling.

"Why don't you come and watch a training session next week and see for yourself," Eddie offers.

"That would be great," replies Joe Junior, turning to his mum with a hopeful smile.

"What a wonderful invitation, we would be delighted," agrees Lilly. "And congratulations on making the team, Eddie."

Realising he hasn't told Eddie his name, Joe introduces himself. "I'm Joe but my teammates call me Joe Junior... and this is Max, my best friend." Max looks up at Eddie and barks his own greeting.

"Great to meet you Joe Junior and you too Max." Eddie turns and wheels away.

"Tuesday night at 6pm," he shouts over his shoulder as he heads towards the cake counter.

Tuesday evening arrives and Joe Junior is really looking forward to seeing his new friend again. He is very excited to see Eddie in action.

Joe hears the commotion before he even sees Eddie and his teammates. There is a lot of squealing and laughter coming from the sports hall.

Eddie sees Joe Junior enter and comes racing over to greet him with a huge grin on his face. "So glad you could make it. We are just about to get started."

The first thing Joe Junior notices is the size of the ball. The ball is much bigger than a normal football. Max has spotted this too and is keen to play. "Maybe later," Joe giggles, seeing his dog's excited face.

Each player in the team is sat in a specially adapted electric powerchair with a seatbelt for safety. There is a joystick for controlling the chair that works just like a video game controller.

Attached to each chair is a footguard in front of the players legs that protects them. It also helps them to control the ball.

The 8 players all gather in the centre of the pitch. They form a circle with their Powerchairs, the footguards of each chair touching.

Some players clap, some punch the air and some whoop. On Eddie's count they all shout together "Go Wheels of Steel!!"

What a great team Joe thinks, watching them get started. Everyone is clearly excited about being part of the Wheels of Steel and it reminds him of his team, Durkar Devils.

The training session of the Wheelchair Football team is very similar to Durkar Devils.

They practice ball skills, shooting, defending and passing the ball. Then they finish by playing a game.

With 4 players on each team, it is very fast and looks like so much fun.

As the session comes to a close, Eddie makes his way over to Joe Junior. "Would you like to have a go?" he offers.

Joe jumps at the chance... "Yes please," he replies with excitement.

"We have a spare chair over there in the corner," Eddie points to the unused chair. "Jump in and come and join us on the pitch!!"

Joe runs over to the Powerchair, climbs in and his Mum helps him to put on the seatbelt. Using the joystick on the arm to steer he turns the chair around and runs straight into the bag of spare balls.

It soon becomes clear that it is not as easy as the team are making it look!

Eddie wheels over to help Joe Junior.

It takes him a while to get used to moving the Powerchair around. He is stopping and starting, going in all the wrong directions. It is a very bumpy ride!

Joe Junior is concentrating so hard that he hasn't even noticed that all the players have stopped to watch him. Eddie and his teammates can't stop laughing... Joe does look funny.

"Don't worry," says Eddie, "it does take a bit of practice. Let's have a go with a ball."

Eddie collects one of the big footballs with the front of his footguard and nudges it into the path of Joe Junior's chair. "Now just push it forwards and try to keep it straight," he instructs.

Joe is surprised to find himself moving quickly forwards and getting close to goal. "Try scoring," Eddie calls from behind him.

With a big nudge Joe pushes the ball towards the goal. To his delight the ball rolls past the defender and over the line.

"Goal!!" he shouts spinning his chair around.

"Great job, Joe..." Eddie says encouragingly, "you have done brilliantly for your first go."

Joe Junior wheels himself over to Eddie and his teammates. "Thank you so much for letting me have a go. I had so much fun."

"You are welcome anytime," replies Eddie with a warm smile. "Why don't you join us for our team chant?"

They all make a circle again, this time with Joe Junior as part of the team. Max the dog comes bounding over to join in.

Footguards touching they all wait for Eddie's count. One, Two, Three...

Laughing and smiling they all shout in their loudest voices possible, "Go Wheels of Steel."

Joe Junior can't wait to see his Durkar Devils teammates again to tell them all about Eddie and his Wheels of Steel.

Joe Junior

supports **Flying School**

LOOK OUT FOR 

Joe Junior and the Dream Team

Joe Junior and his New Teammate

Joe Junior and the Grand Opening

Joe Junior, the Internet Sensation

Joe Junior and the Floating Pitch

Joe Junior and the Secret Prince

ABOUT THE AUTHOR

Carol has been a football fan since she was Joe Junior's age. She turned her love of football into a career, working for the Football Association for 16 years. As a Team Operations Manager, Carol helped support the England National Football Teams at all levels working at numerous World Cups, European Championships and as Team Manager for the Team GB Men's Football Team for the 2012 Olympic Games. Still working within the game Carol continues to find new adventures for Joe Junior to enjoy.

Printed in Great Britain
by Amazon

52933394R00023